Head of Blind-worm. 1/2

A Book=scorpion (*Chelifer can-croides*). 5/1

Click-beetle, natural size.

Sinea diadema, one of the *Reduviidæ*. (Line shows natural size.)

a. Cotton=stainer

Proxys punctulatus.

Hellgrammite (*a*) and Hellgrammite-fly.

The Bait=bug.

Epeiridæ.
a, male, and *b*, female, of *Epeira stellata*; *c*, characteristic orb=web of an epeirid (*Epeira strix*).

Parasite of the Beaver (*Platy-psyllus castoris*). (Line shows natural size.)

Rose-beetle (*Cetonia aurata*). Vertical line shows natural size.

Agonoderus dorsalis (Le Conte). Vertical line shows natural size.

The Twig=girdler (*Oncideres cingulata*). 1/1 *a*, a branch girdled by the beetle.

The I Drag (*Dra eatus*

Hawthorn-tingis *arcuata*), one of th enlarged about ten

Flour-beetle (*T litor*). (Line sh size.)

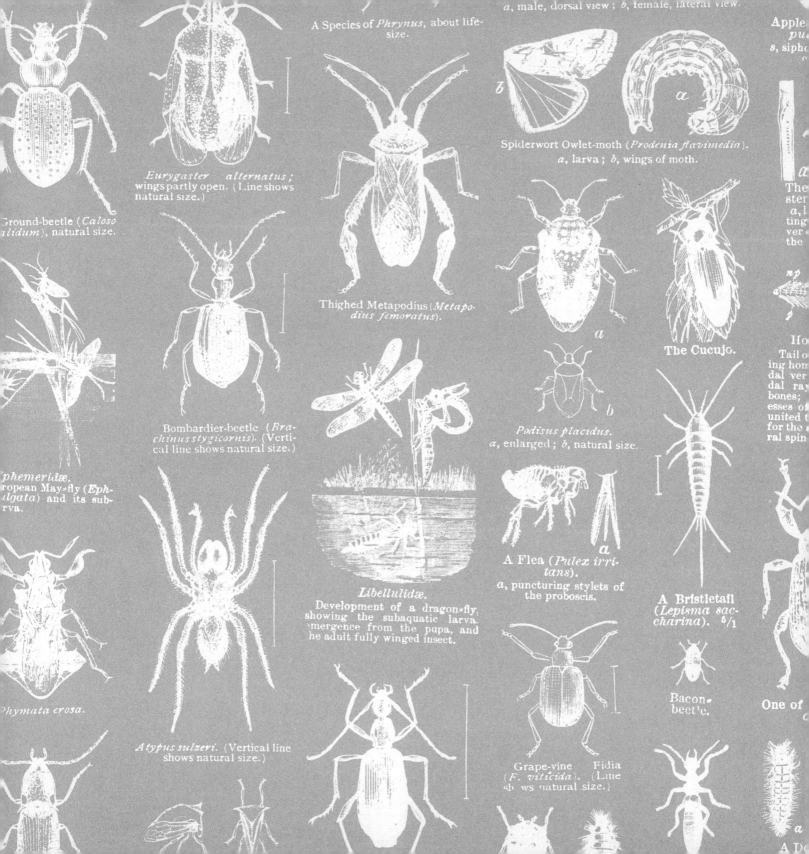

Ground-beetle (*Caloso
 ilidum*), natural size.

Eurygaster alternatus;
wings partly open. (Line shows
natural size.)

A Species of *Phrynus*, about life-
size.

a, male, dorsal view ; *b*, female, lateral view.

Spiderwort Owlet-moth (*Prodenia flavimedia*).
a, larva ; *b*, wings of moth.

Apple
 pu
s, sipho

The
 ster
a, l
ting
ver
the

np

Ho
Tail o
ing hom
dal ver
dal ra
bones;
esses o
united t
for the
ral spin

Thighed Metapodius (*Metapodius femoratus*).

The Cucujo.

phemeridæ.
ropean May-fly (*Eph-
 igata*) and its sub-
rva.

Bombardier-beetle (*Bra-
chinus stygicornis*). (Vertical line shows natural size.)

a

b

Podisus placidus.
a, enlarged ; *b*, natural size.

Libellulidæ.
Development of a dragon-fly,
showing the subaquatic larva,
 mergence from the pupa, and
he adult fully winged insect.

a

A Flea (*Pulex irri-
tans*).
a, puncturing stylets of
the proboscis.

A Bristletail
(*Lepisma sac-
charina*). ⁵/₁

Phymata erosa.

Atypus sulzeri. (Vertical line
shows natural size.)

Bacon-
beet'e.

One of

Grape-vine Fidia
(*F. viticida*). (Line
sh ws natural size.)

ant

by

Ting Morris

illustrated by

Desiderio Sanzi

designed by

Deb Miner

W
FRANKLIN WATTS
LONDON•SYDNEY

Who will you meet on your walk through the woods today?

Listen. Can you hear a rustling sound?

Look. Can you see tiny creatures carrying leaves along the forest floor?

Turn the page and take a closer look.

It is just getting light in the woods, and all the plants are covered with dew. There is a neat pile of pine needles, twigs and earth in the undergrowth. **This is the home of a colony of wood ants.**

But on this chilly spring morning there seems to be no one about. Perhaps all the ants are inside the nest. **Can you see any?**

THE NEST

A wood ants' nest can be up to 2 metres high and 4 metres across. About half a million ants usually live in a colony. Some nests have room for as many as three million ants.

OTHER ANT HOMES

 Garden ants feel safe and warm under a large flat stone, concrete slab or brick.

 Some ants make their nests in rotten logs or inside plants.

Weaver ants build tree homes. They stick the edges of two leaves together with silk threads made by their grubs. Each ant builder carries a grub in its jaws and uses it like a tube of glue.

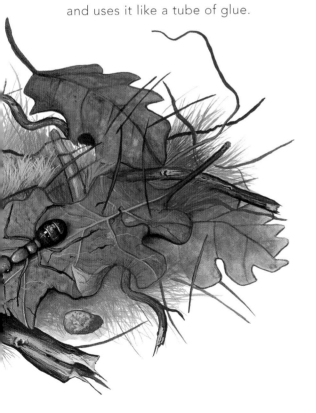

AN ANT'S BODY

An ant's body has three parts: the HEAD, the THORAX and the ABDOMEN.

An ant has six legs, with two hooked CLAWS at the end of each one. On each front LEG there are two COMBS. The ant uses these to clean its other legs and its FEELERS (or antennae).

The feelers are used to smell, touch, taste and hear.

Ants have two EYES, but they can't see very well. Some kinds of ants are blind.

An ant's mouth has strong JAWS for cutting up food, biting enemies and carrying things.

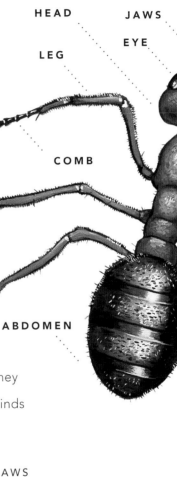

FEELERS

HEAD   JAWS

EYE

LEG

COMB

THORAX

ABDOMEN

CLAW

Now that the sun is shining, it feels warm in the forest.

Inside the nest, the ants pass messages to each other. The underground tunnels are coming alive, and suddenly thousands of ants emerge. **They are soaking up the heat after the long, cold winter.** They seem to go in and out as if they are on duty. But what are their duties, and how do they know what to do?

WARMING AND COOLING

Ants control the temperature inside their nest. After a cold spell, they go outside to soak up the sun's heat, and then go back in to warm up the nest.

On a hot day the sun warms the anthill. If it becomes too hot, the ants open small holes at the top to let in air. At night, they close the holes with soil and pine needles.

WHO LIVES IN THE COLONY?

Ants live together in colonies. They are called social insects because they have different duties and they all share the work. In the nest, there are three kinds of wood ants.

THE QUEEN She is the largest ant and the only one in the colony that can lay eggs. All the other ants depend on her.

8

WORKERS They are small female ants that do everything from building the nest to nursing young ants.

MALES Their only job is to fertilize the queen during her mating flight. That is why they grow wings. They cannot feed themselves and soon starve.

9

The queen has told her nursery ants that she is ready to start laying eggs. She needs more room, more warmth, more air and more food. The queen likes sweet-tasting foods, and sometimes the workers have to go a long way to keep her happy.

Can you help this worker feed the queen? Use your finger to find a way through the maze of tunnels.

NEST CHAMBERS

Inside the nest there are lots of rooms and tunnels – the queen's chamber, nurseries, rooms for storing food, and even a rubbish heap. The ants spend the winter in the deepest rooms underground.

GETTING THE MESSAGE

Ants talk to each other by making special chemicals that other ants can smell. They give off different smells to tell each other about food, enemies and nest duties. Ants pick up the scent with their feelers. When two ants tap feelers, they are talking to each other.

Ants from a different colony smell different, so it's easy to recognize outsiders.

RUBBISH HEAP

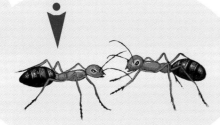

ROYAL MESSENGER

The queen stays in touch with all the workers through her nursery ants. She gives out liquid messages on her body, which they lick off her and pass around the colony.

BRUSHING UP

Before feeding the queen, worker ants clean themselves by brushing off dirt from the outside world.

ROYAL CHAMBER

A column of ants is marching through the woods in search of food. Now that the queen's eggs are hatching and the brood is growing, there are many more mouths to feed. News about some exciting food has reached the nest, and workers are on their way to bring it back. **What will they find?** Perhaps some tiny crumbs left behind after a picnic in the woods.

HELPERS NEEDED

Ants use teamwork. When an ant comes back to the nest with news about food, it wiggles its feelers, butts heads with other ants, and spits out some of the food it has found. Helpers quickly find their way to the food by following a scent trail laid by their fellow workers or by holding on to the leader's hind legs with their feelers. Young ants that can't keep up or get lost along the way are carried by other workers.

MUSCLE POWER

Ants eat plants, seeds and other insects. Wood ants sometimes capture wasps and flies. Workers are very strong and can carry things that weigh much more than they do.

HUNTING FOR FOOD

Looking for food outside the nest is a dangerous job. Only older wood ants go on foraging trips. Birds, frogs and spiders are all enemies, and sometimes ants have to fight rival ant colonies. People can be a danger too – they might step on an ant without noticing it.

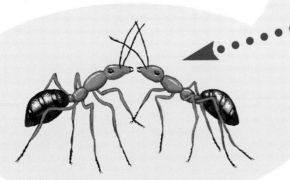

MOUTH TO MOUTH

An ant carries food by storing it in a pouch in its stomach called a crop. Then it shares it with other ants back in the nest. The feeder passes chewed-up food into the mouth of a hungry ant. If the ant wants more food, it strokes the feeder's head with its feelers.

13

Ants like sweet-tasting food, and this tree is full of goodies. The wood ants lick the sticky sap from the bark and catch tiny insects that live under it. High up in the branches, they keep herds of insects called aphids, and milk them like farmers. The ants stroke the aphids and drink the droplets of sweet honeydew that come out of them. This delicious sugary drink is full of vitamins and is a special treat to take back for the grubs in the nest.

ANT GARDENERS

Leaf-cutter ants grow their own food – a large grey fungus. First, workers gather leaves and carry them to the underground 'garden' in their nest. There, ant gardeners chew them up and put the pulp on the fungus to make it grow. They weed the garden and have special heaps for their rubbish and dead ants. All the ants in the colony eat the fungus.

GOOD FARMERS

Aphids are insects which live on plants. They suck the sap from plants, and some of this sap comes out of the aphids as sugar. Ants milk aphids by tapping the insects' backs with their feelers. They drink the honeydew, then spit it back up to feed the larvae, or grubs, in the nest.

Ants protect aphids from other enemies. They carry them to safety and sometimes even take them into their nest. There they keep them on roots that grow through an underground room.

NEST GUESTS

Ants often share their nest with other small creatures. These might be woodlice, beetles, spiders, mites or millipedes. The caterpillar of the blue butterfly gives out a sweet liquid that ants love to drink.

Some tiny ants may build their own nest inside a wood ant home. When the wood ants move to a new area, these ants follow them.

HONEY POTS

Some kinds of ants, called honey-pot ants, store liquid food in a special way. They feed their workers with honeydew. The workers then swell up and are used as storage pots for the whole colony. They hang from their feet in the nest and give out food whenever they are tapped.

15

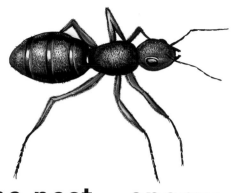

There's alarm in the nest – enemy ants are coming! At the entrance, guards are fighting the first intruders. The guards tap with their legs and send out smells to warn the ants inside. Nursery workers move the grubs to a safe place, while others go to join the fight.

They grab the enemy ants' legs and feelers, hold them down, and squirt poison at them. The dead ants are dragged away. The wood ants have won the battle and saved their nest.

ON THE MARCH

Army ants have very strong jaws. Thousands of ants march in long columns and eat any other insects or spiders they come across.

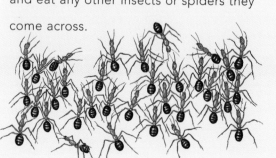

WATCH OUT!

The red garden ant has a nasty sting that is painful to humans. Never pick one up with your fingers.

ALARM BELLS

When an ant spots an enemy, it stands like this and gives off an alarm chemical to warn its nest-mates. During the fight, it makes more alarm smells to call other fighters.

BIG HEADS

Some ant colonies have soldiers with big heads, which they use to block the nest entrance. The soldiers open the door only to their own workers with the right smell. Their big heads are also very useful for pushing enemies out of the nest.

FIGHTING AND BITING

Ants protect themselves by stinging or biting. The poison that comes out of an ant's sharp sting can kill other insects. A wood ant does not have a sting, but squirts a poison called formic acid. It bites its enemy, bends its abdomen between its legs and squirts poison into the wound.

17

Feed me! Clean my eggs! Take them to a warm place! Hurry, hurry! These are the queen's orders. **It is hot today, but there's no time for the nursery workers to relax in the sunshine.**

They are busy all the time, licking

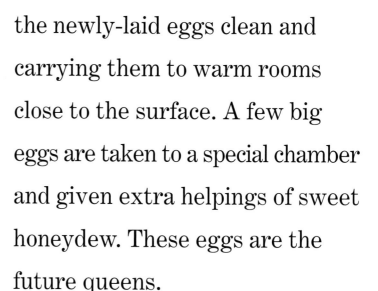

● **NO SLEEP**
Ants never sleep, but they take little rests. Special chambers in a nest are used as resting places for the nursery workers.

the newly-laid eggs clean and carrying them to warm rooms close to the surface. A few big eggs are taken to a special chamber and given extra helpings of sweet honeydew. These eggs are the future queens.

BROTHERS AND SISTERS

The queen lays her eggs during spring and summer. She is the mother of all the ants in the nest. Most of them will become female worker ants, but some will become male ants with wings. Nursery workers lick a few large eggs to pass on honeydew, which feeds the eggs and helps them grow. These lucky few will become young queens with wings.

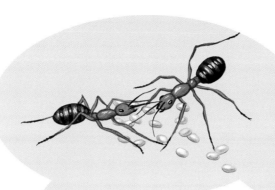

NURSERIES

There are several nurseries in the nest. Nursery workers keep the eggs warm and clean. If a room becomes too cold or too wet, they move the eggs. If there is a frost, they take the eggs to chambers deep underground.

ANT EGGS

Eggs that hold worker ants are oval and measure about half a millimetre. Eggs that contain queens are much larger.

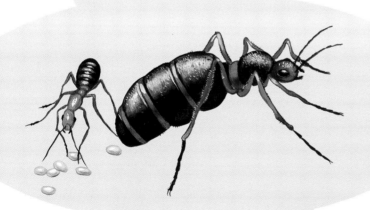

HOW ANTS DEVELOP

Ants go through four stages of development.

1 EGG

The eggs are small – about half a millimetre long.

2 LARVA

After a few days, the eggs hatch into larvae, or grubs. Nursery ants feed them. When the grubs are three to five millimetres long, they change again.

3 PUPA

Each larva spins a silk cocoon around itself. Inside the cocoon, it grows into a pupa, or young ant. Nursery ants carry the cocoons up into a sunny spot so they develop more quickly. This stage lasts about three weeks.

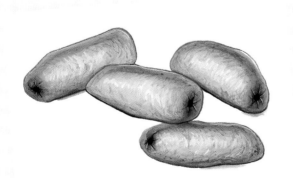

Look what's happening in the nursery. **The young ants are ready to come out of their cocoons.** But some are too weak to chew their way out. Nursery ants are helping them to struggle free. These pale little ants can't even walk, but in a few weeks' time they will be strong enough to join the workers.

4 ANT

When they come out of their cocoons, young ants are pale and cannot walk properly. They are fed and looked after by the nursery ants for another few weeks.

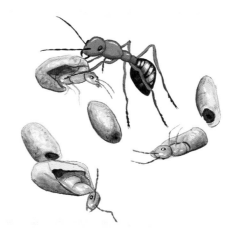

It's a hot, damp summer's day. A young queen is leaving her nest. She spreads her wings and flies high into the sky. Suddenly the air is buzzing with flying ants coming out of the ground. They are male ants from other nests who want to find a queen and mate with her. Today, all the wood ant queens in this forest are on their mating flight. **Have you ever seen flying ants?**

A SHORT LIFE

Male ants live for only a few weeks. They can't feed themselves, and they are fed by female workers until their mating flight. After the flight, they are not allowed back into the nest, and they die within a few days.

BORN WORKERS

A worker's life is hard and dangerous. Workers live for up to five years.

22

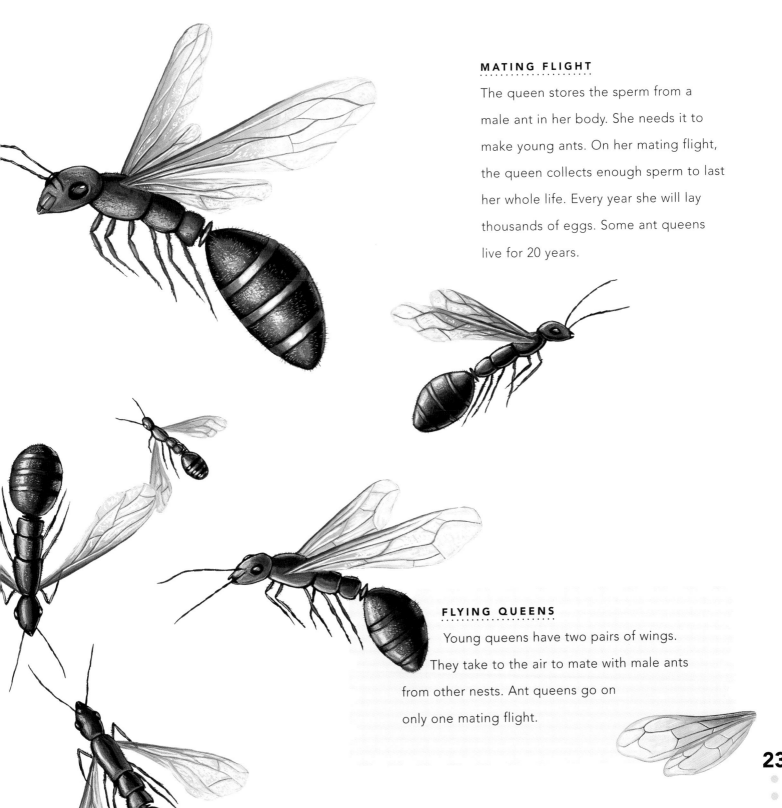

MATING FLIGHT

The queen stores the sperm from a male ant in her body. She needs it to make young ants. On her mating flight, the queen collects enough sperm to last her whole life. Every year she will lay thousands of eggs. Some ant queens live for 20 years.

FLYING QUEENS

Young queens have two pairs of wings. They take to the air to mate with male ants from other nests. Ant queens go on only one mating flight.

A young wood ant queen has landed and is searching for a good nesting site. She wants a safe, warm place to lay her eggs. Once she finds it, she bites off her wings – she won't need them again – and digs a hole. Then she covers herself up in her small underground chamber. Here the queen will lay her eggs and start a new colony of wood ants.

AMAZON ANTS

An Amazon ant queen lays her eggs in another colony's nest. She kills the old queen, and the workers become hers and look after her.

NEW COLONY

When the queen starts a new colony, she has no helpers to look after her, so she lives off fat in her body. When her eggs hatch, she feeds the young grubs herself. But once the first ants are strong enough to help, they do all the work. The queen never leaves the nest again.

Now look back at the picture on page 9. Within a year, the queen's new colony will be crawling with thousands of ants. It will be a big mound with many underground rooms.

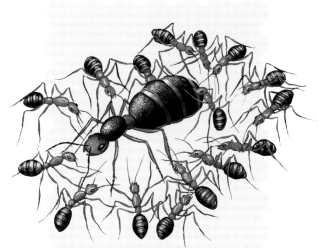

SOLDIER QUEEN

Army ants don't build a nest, because they are always on the march. When their queen is ready to lay her eggs, the workers stop and crowd around her. Within 20 days, the eggs will grow into young ants ready to march on.

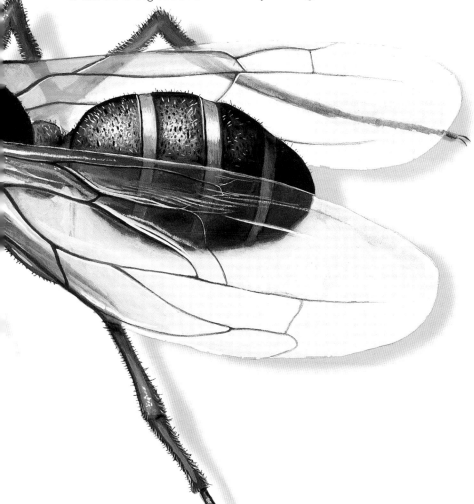

The queen ant
lays eggs.

Ant

The queen mates
with a male ant.

Most of the ants
become workers.

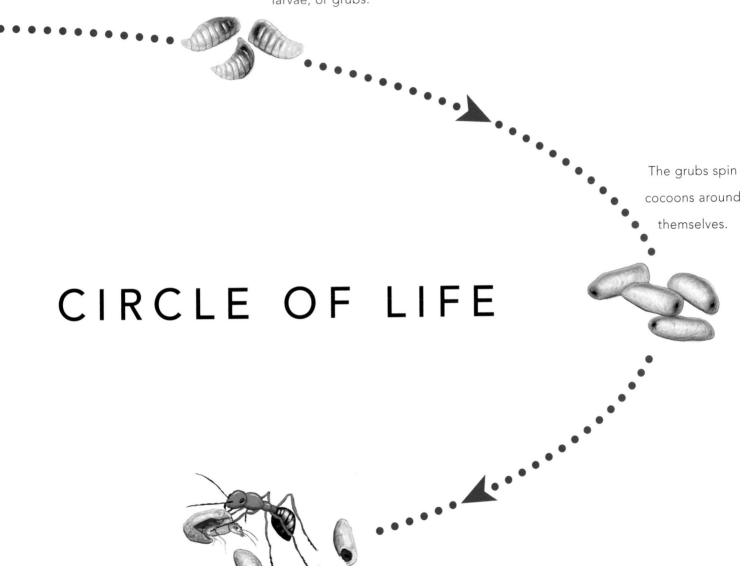

The eggs hatch into larvae, or grubs.

The grubs spin cocoons around themselves.

CIRCLE OF LIFE

The ants emerge from their cocoons.

brood A large group of young.

chamber A room in a nest.

cocoons Silky cases spun by insect larvae, which protect them while they grow into pupae.

colony A large group of animals that live close together as a community.

fertilize To cause a female insect's eggs to develop into young.

foraging Searching for food.

fungus One of a group of very simple living things, such as moulds and mushrooms.

grubs The young form of some insects; another word for larvae.

mate To come together to make young.

mating flight A flight made by winged queen ants when they mate with male ants.

millipedes Small creatures with long, thin bodies and many legs.

mites Tiny, eight-legged creatures related to spiders.

nursing Caring for young; nursery ants take care of young ants.

sap The juice inside a plant that serves as its food.

sperm Fluid produced by male animals that makes a female's eggs grow into young.

vitamins Substances found in food that animals need to be healthy.

 An Appleseed Editions book

First published in 2004 by Franklin Watts
96 Leonard Street, London, EC2A 4XD

Franklin Watts Australia
45–51 Huntley Street, Alexandria, NSW 2015

© 2004 Appleseed Editions

Created by Appleseed Editions Ltd,
Well House, Friars Hill, Guestling, East Sussex, TN35 4ET

Illustrator: Desiderio Sanzi

Designer: Deb Miner

ISBN 0 7496 5701 4

A CIP catalogue for this book is available from the British Library.

Printed and bound in the USA

Markings.

raonis). 4/1   *nalis*). 3/1

Head of Blind-
worm. 1/2

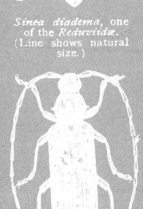

A Book-scorpion
(*Chelifer can-
croides*). 5/1

a
Cotton-stainer

Epeiridæ.
a, male, and *b*, fe-
male, of *Epeira stel-
lata; c*, characteristic
orb-web of an epeirid
(*Epeira strix*).

The Dr
Dragon
(*Drac
eatus*).

Click-beetle,
natural size.

Proxys punctulatus.

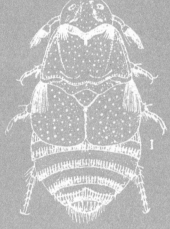

Parasite of the Beaver (*Platy-
psyllus castoris*). (Line shows
natural size.)

Agonoderus dorsalis (Le Conte).
Vertical line shows natural size.

Hawthorn-tingis
arcuata), one of the
enlarged about ten ti

a

Hellgrammite (*a*)
and Hellgrammite-
fly.

The Twig-gir-
dler (*Oncideres
cingulata*). 1/1
a, a branch girdled by the beetle.

Sinea diadema, one
of the *Reduviidæ.*
(Line shows natural
size.)

The Bait-bug.

Rose-beetle (*Cetonia aurata*).
Vertical line shows natural size.

Flour-beetle (*Te
litor*). (Line sho
size.)

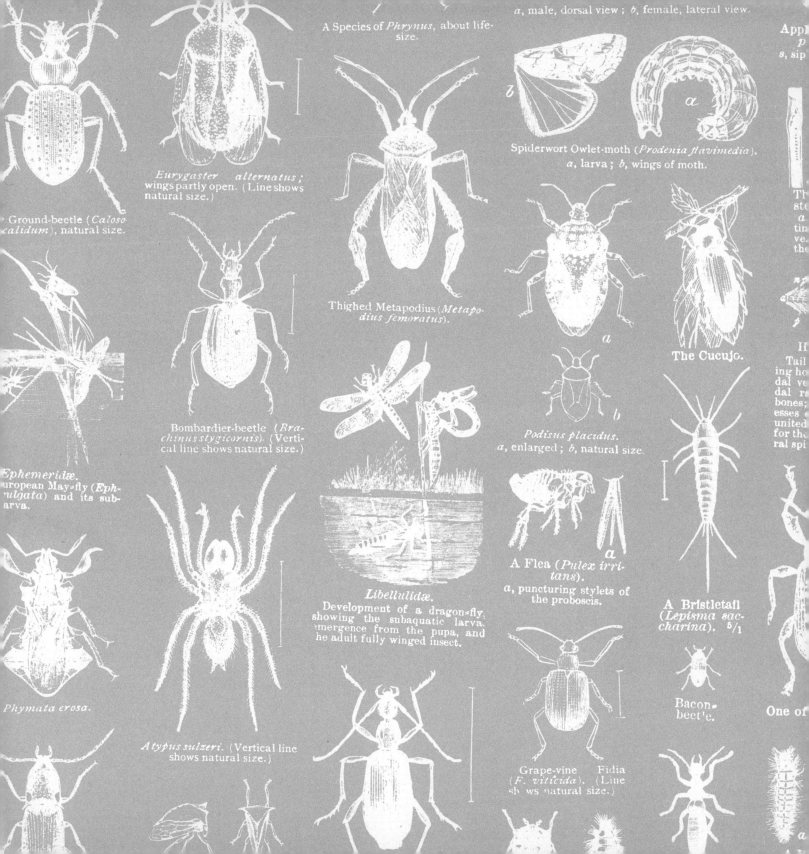

Ground-beetle (*Caloso calidum*), natural size.

Eurygaster alternatus; wings partly open. (Line shows natural size.)

A Species of *Phrynus*, about life-size.

a, male, dorsal view; *b*, female, lateral view.

Spiderwort Owlet-moth (*Prodenia flavimedia*). *a*, larva; *b*, wings of moth.

Thighed Metapodius (*Metapodius femoratus*).

The Cucujo.

Ephemeridæ. European May-fly (*Ephemera vulgata*) and its sub-larva.

Bombardier-beetle (*Brachinus stygicornis*). (Vertical line shows natural size.)

Podisus placidus. a, enlarged; *b*, natural size.

Libellulidæ. Development of a dragon-fly, showing the subaquatic larva, emergence from the pupa, and the adult fully winged insect.

A Flea (*Pulex irritans*). *a*, puncturing stylets of the proboscis.

A Bristletail (*Lepisma saccharina*). 5/1

Phymata erosa.

Atypus sulzeri. (Vertical line shows natural size.)

Bacon-beetle.

Grape-vine Fidia (*F. viticida*). (Line shows natural size.)